Cover Design & Photos by Domenic Fusco
Edited by Charlie Fusco & Giovannina V. Fusco Suluh

A Ministry Guide for Producing Powerful Video

Copyright © 2002, 2011, 2014
Domenic Fusco

Published by arrangement with Visible Light Ministries, Inc.

ISBN-13: 978-1502553638
ISBN-10: 1502553635

For information contact:

Visible Light, Inc.
P. O. Box 4200
Sanford FL 32772
www.visiblelight.org

Printed in the U.S.A.

A MINISTRY GUIDE FOR

Producing

Powerful
Video

Proven Steps for Success

by **Domenic Fusco**

2

To my wife, Charlie, whose literary skill, artistic talent, and never ending support made this book a reality. And to my wonderful daughter who has always been a delight. She never ceases to use her exceptional talents to make me look good!

"The only way for a man to give birth is to create art."
Sava Shalman
St. Petersburg, Russia

Introduction

I have yet to meet anyone with a more adventurous and colorful childhood than I experienced. Every six months my mother would flip a coin, "heads we clean, tails we move." Ten different schools by the time I graduated from high school gave me a *real* education. Those experiences—the life skills gained— mean more today than my high school diploma or college degrees. By the way I am the one in the middle.

I remember when I was ten years old; mom picked up my two brothers and me at boarding school. She said we were going to Las Vegas. At that time, Nevada was the only state in the USA that would grant a divorce in six months. She was with a man who was driving a big, brand new red Eldorado convertible. Wanted by the FBI, it turned out our chauffeur and Mom's new "friend" was the infamous "Cigar Bandit". On our trip out West, he robbed banks from NY to Las Vegas lighting the dynamite sticks with his cigar. I still have in my possession a Movado watch he gave me, stolen somewhere between St Louis and Denver. I was told it was worth $1500 at the time (1955).

And what does all of this have to do with video? Well, videos are stories, and I attribute my success in the wonderful world of video to the experiences of my youth; my ability to tell stories. My *passion to create* and the *power of imagination* was developed while enjoying long hours of freedom as a child. Growing up in the 40's and 50's without the constant input of television allowed us to dream... to imagine. I attribute my *empathetic sensitivity* to the many cultures I adopted growing up in New York City. My *love of fellowman* came as a result of the pain of a broken family. And finally, my *thirst for knowledge and my desire to share it* was nurtured during my youthful travels and adjustment to develop new relationships in every new neighborhood.

Whether making friends in a new town or creating a powerful video, one must be an observer of life, a lover of mankind and the teller of ageless stories in an ever-changing world. May all your stories have "happy ever after endings".

Domenic Fusco

If only I had a copy of the "**Quick Guide for Producing Powerful Video**" two decades ago!

Over the last twenty years, I have produced literally hundreds of videos with budgets ranging from a few hundred dollars into the tens of thousands of dollars. Whether producing a promotional, corporate image, "how-to", employee training or any number of other uses for video*, there is no substitute for knowledge and experience*. Within these pages are years of knowledge and first-hand experience which will give you the tools needed to better understand and implement the skills of video production. For the professional producer, it's a good reminder of how to do the basics well and maybe even learn something new that we hadn't thought of before. No matter what your level of experience is, you will find this book a valuable resource for your next production.

Richard Germaine,

Independent Producer & Marketing Consultant

http://www.richgermaine.com/

Preface

I have been successfully producing media for corporate and Christian organizations for four decades. It is my absolute passion to bring the message of Christ to the nations through the media arts! I love the process of meeting new people, creatively telling their stories and insights, and of course, the spiritual rewards that come with serving God and mankind.

Without a doubt, this book is a fast-track to honing the skills to create effective media productions. The content provides the education, pre-production basics, branding, and marketing techniques I have employed to sell and produce highly effective video presentations and website media. As I approach a new chapter in my life, I would like to pass this knowledge on to those in ministry, as well as those who are considering or have chosen video production as a career. I am sure the contents will help you develop impacting presentations to reach your audience.

Although this book was originally written for students and entrepreneurs in the media field (*A Quick Guide for Producing Powerful Video*), the content is rooted in a Biblical world view. My attitude and actions in a secular setting are no less tied to my faith than my ministry efforts. I prayerfully undertake each new project as doing it unto the Lord; my highest priority is emulating the character of Christ in a spirit of excellence for His glory.

This book does not cite scriptural references in support of the shared principles. Rather, the emphasis is on technique rather than substance of message. Corporate examples are used which apply to Christian media campaigns as well: all should be approached as doing the work of the Kingdom.

I encourage you to read another of my books - *The Articles of Transformation* - and to utilize the accompanying *Personal Discovery Journal* in pursuit of Christian character principles. They are the stepping stones to success in the market place, ministry, and every area of your private life and relationships. I trust that this transformational series will enhance your life and increase your ministry effectiveness.

May God bless you richly in your calling!

Domenic Fusco

Partial Lists for Profit and Non-Profit Clients

From the Kremlin to Kalamzoo, Siberia to South Beach, Italy to Israel, Africa to Amsterdam, and Canada to Cozemel, Image Artistry has produced award-winning promotional videos, training series, TV Ads, sales and PR campaigns, inspirational videos and documentaries for industry leaders.

In the corporate world
it's referred to as
Branding....
Marketing...
Selling for Success!

In the cosmos of entertainment it's
Creative Story Telling...
Emotionally Connecting...
Cultivating Excitement for Applause!

In either case the end game is to
Move Your Audience...
Satisfy Their Appetites...
And Have Them Clamoring for More.

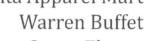

Stone Mountain Park
Atlanta Apparel Mart
Warren Buffet
Seven Eleven
Chevron
Marriott
C-SPAN
CNN
IBM
HBO
Super Bowl
Life Time Cable
Nissan
Applebees
Ferrari
Easter Seals
Emory University
Stirling/Sotheby's
Hank Aaron
Azurix
ComAir
Lafarge
UpJohn
Bell South
Poly Portables
Redzee
Evander Holyfield

CEEC
MovieGuide
Logos Global Network
CRU (Campus Crusade for Christ)
Dave Neathery Ministries
Mountain Top Entertainment
South Pass the Musical
Easter Seals
Horse Whisperer
Christian Retreat/Gerald Derstine
CBN
Peninsular FL District, AOG
International Prison Ministry
PTL
Christian Prison Ministries
Mike Atkins Ministries
Christian Sportsmen Fellowship, Intl.
Jack Murphy Ministries
COPE
Israel Affairs International
House of Hope
Bridges of America
TBN
Bill Glass Ministries
New Tribes Mission
International Seminary
Hosanna Ministries
Fish House Ministries
Call for Hope
Charisma/Ministries
Craig Marlatt Ministries
Linda Gove Ministries
Churches/Ministries Globally

Table of Contents

Introduction

1 **The Digital Revolution**
    The Steps for Creating Visual Media
    have been turned Upside Down

2 **The A's of Pre-Production**
    Required to Produce Powerful Video Presentations

3 **The B's of Pre-Production**
    Every Great Presentation Contains these Elements

4 **The C's of Pre-Production**
    Three Necessary Steps to Success

5 **Production Steps to Success**
    The Basic Flow and Steps of Producing a Video

6 **How to Choose the Best Production Co.**
    What to Look For and the Right Questions to Ask

7 **No One Person is a Team**
    Your Contribution to a Successful Video

Today knowledge has power. It controls access to opportunity and advancement.

Peter F. Drucker

The Digital Revolution

The sequence for creating visual
media has been turned ǝpᴉsd∩-uʍop.

The Digital Revolution

Change... it is the only constant. We have to deal with change everyday in our quest to assist corporate America in selling more products, training employees to perform with greater skill and positioning new discoveries in the consumer markets of the world. Godly principles do not change but our approach and delivery does change.

Change brings us the **DIGITAL REVOLUTION**. New digital formats and media have an enormous impact on every aspect of society and has delightfully forced innovation on the world of visual media. Video has improved so much that Hollywood *films* are now being produced on *video* (The **RED ONE** has been upgraded to the **EPIC** which surpasses the quality of film). Filmmakers such as George Lucas are taking full advantage of this new technology. This technology is becoming increasingly affordable and will soon replace the traditional movie-goer's experience as theaters convert from film projection to downloaded digital signals. In some areas, the change has already begun.

Most importantly, corporate America and the Church has the ability to use the advances in *digital* media to get their message to millions of potential clients with expedience and less expense than ever before imagined. Now potential customers can instantly watch a high quality promotional video presentation delivered via the Internet anywhere in the world. Preachers can share the Gospel with millions.

Presentations can be produced in a fraction of the time and at a fraction of the cost of just ten years ago. The process has been simplified. Footage is first captured on a high-resolution *digital* video camera then edited using a *digital* non-linear editing suite. Presentations can be enhanced with 2D and 3D computer graphics and then played back in a variety of ways: Internet streaming, thumb nail drive, DVD and more. Although an office may not have a video player, it is almost a sure thing it has a computer which provides instant access to your presentation!

Video Cameras are now used for Photography

The RED EPIC shoots 30 photos a second in the highest format imaginable. Photographers are using these video cameras instead of the classical photo cameras. These photo frames can be used in all your media projects as illustrated on the following pages.

In 1996 I wrote we would someday see the end of TV and all visual media would be seen on CV (computer vision). It is coming to pass every day with the internet as the delivery system. Many people are canceling their cable and view television programming on the internet.

Impact of the Internet

The **Internet** is a global system of interconnected computer networks that use the standard Internet protocol suite (TCP/IP) to serve several billion users worldwide. It is a *network of networks* that consists of millions of private, public, academic, business, and government networks, of local to global scope, that are linked by a broad array of electronic, wireless, and optical networking technologies.

The emergence of social networks like **Face Book, Twitter, Pinterest, LinkedIn, Instagram** have accelerated the need for visual media, not the least of which is video.

Low cost videos are posted by clients on their Face Book sites. The client profits greatly from this low cost advertizing venue and they enjoy immediate research free feedback.

Video Web Sites

Here are five of the top video websites that generate more than a billion new contacts each month. That was a billion *NEW* contact, not million! This proves the demand for video is growing daily.

Video Stock Libraries

I have shot video around the world for the past thirty plus years. In doing so I accumulated and library of stock footage that supports my production needs. Every clip is digitized and available at the click of my mouse. But as you can imagine things change. We now produce 16 by 9 formats instead of 4 by 3. Soon we will be required to produce 4K (4000 pixels wide) instead of HD 2K (1920 wide). I recently had a project that needed special footage and bought clips from a source that was so reasonable, I would have had to spend 1000 times the money to shoot the footage myself. The point is you can create even more powerful video for all kinds of clients and projects at a fraction of the cost thanks to the digital revolution.

Smart Phones

Look around and you will be amazed at how many smart phones are shooting HD video and posting it on the internet. Those shooters will certainly never replace the talent needed to produce power video presentations. The commercial world needs more than paint, a brush and canvas to be a great artist. But the use of video is growing beyond the imagination of the last century's masses. A video posted on the internet once copied and transferred will be around forever. You can't take it back. People have been fired within hours after video of their activities have been posted. And now we have Dick Tracy video phones!!!

Video Production is not an expense!

It is an investment. The bottom line matters in Hollywood your company and the Church. Some questions to ponder:

What would be the return on your investment over the next six months or year for a sales video?

If a new promotional video is used at a trade show, how many new customers would be developed?

How many more systems would you sell?

If a new and efficient manufacturing process is developed in your division how much money would other divisions save by sharing the process on video?

How much better would the sales force perform in front of a potential customer after watching a training video on the benefits of a new product?

If the answers seem obvious, use this book to conceptualize, formalize and produce your next video.

This Quick-Guide is designed to educate and assist you with practical application of knowledge acquired over the past thirty years of production. The principles, experience and techniques when applied will result in the production of powerful video that will perform as designed.

The next two pages illustrate how video can be used to produce many of your media needs. Think about it!

You might consider using video for...

PHOTOS

There are 30 frames or pictures for each second of video. On a digital editing suite you are able to export any frame as a JPG file and you have a photo! The photos can be used for 3, 4, 5, 6 and 7. The only limitation is size (3 to 4 inches wide at 300 dpi).

BROCHURE

Once your video promotional is done the creative copy and photos taken from the video footage can be made into a high impact corporate print brochure. This approach assures that a cohesive image is maintained with all your media.

WEB SITE

Just imagine your video presentation on the internet. And, by now you realize the photos needed for your internet site can be derived from your video clips. This approach maintains your corporate image, an added benefit of producing video first!

5

DATA SHEETS

Company Information and photos are simply extracted from video footage and can be added to your data to create your data Sheets required for customer collateral. Whether it is a data sheet, new product release or ad slick it begins with creating a video presentation.

6

PRESS SHEETS

If you have read 2, 3, 4 and 5 it is easy to understand how to create a Press Sheet or Press Release from your video presentation. You save time and money by simply producing a video Promotional first then using the photos and creative copy!

7

YOUTUBE & WEB

Here is one of the most exciting new mediums to sell a vision, product or service. Interact with pages of print and of course actual video footage right from you computer. And social networks are now a must in the corporate world.

Meticulous planning will enable everything a man does to appear spontaneous.

Mark Caine

The Four Essential Steps
Required to Produce
Powerful Video Presentations

My baseball coach insisted that the game was won before we even entered the stadium. What we thought about our performance was indeed a deciding factor in the outcome of the actual game. *"You win before you begin,"* he'd always say. This is a proven fact! Former Atlanta Braves pitcher, John Smoltz, regularly works on his game with the help of a psychologist. This has resulted in his overcoming former obstacles that mentally hindered his physical performance. The results speak for themselves. Not only has this technique proven effective in baseball, but also in other professional and amateur sports such as basketball where players visualize or mentally rehearse successfully shooting foul shots. The players who utilize this technique increase their game shooting averages over players who practice only on the court. *Visualizing success is a critical factor in winning the game.*

So, what does this have to do with video productions? To create a successful video presentation, you must create every detail of the project in your mind and on the drawing board in detail before it comes to realization. The famous football coach, Vince Lombardi, taught that "whoever best executes the fundamentals wins the game." The fundamentals of producing a successful video or film presentation begins with planning. Start by creating a vision of your objective or **AIM**. This must be followed by defining your **AUDIENCE** (demographic, psychographic, geographic, etc.). Next, you should carefully consider the **APPROACH** that will present your project with clarity and impact to your specific audience. Finally, discern the necessary factors required to motivate your target market/audience toward the **ACTION** you desire. These are just a few of the steps to be taken before you begin production.

The A's of Production

There is no substitution for planning or avision. You need a point on the horizon to walk toward. And there is nothing more important than the A's in creating your presentation. In fact they will work for a teacher, preacher, producer or anyone who desires to communicate effectively. Every successful video presentation will have these elements well defined, if not on paper, then in mind. I request that my clients take time to well define each of the A's—for my benefit as well as their benefit. This exercise never fails to create a product the customer is most pleased with, but also a production that achieves the aim. If you were to read only one chapter in The Quick Guide to Producing Powerful Video... this is the one!!! Get ready to learn the timeless truths that will be worth their weight in gold. The A's to commit to memory are:

Aim
Audience
Approach
Action

Aim

Begin with a Specific Purpose.

The following examples illustrate the three major goals behind the creation of video for the corporate world. They are effective and essential for the sales and marketing of a company's products, services, and people.

A. A presentation that will help you **IMPROVE** performance and effectiveness.

Improve your position in the market place.
Improve a bad or faltering image.
Improve comprehension of service and/or
     product capability.

B. A presentation that will help you **ACHIEVE** learning objectives and develop behavior (personal growth).

Achieve a greater share of marketplace dollars.
Achieve a working knowledge of products or
     services.
Achieve a greater understanding of corporate
     goals.

C. A presentation that will help you **CHANGE** opinions or perceptions.

Change the opinion of product or service
     capabilities.
Change the attitude toward company policies
     or performance.
Change the perception of personnel.

     Your **AIM** or "purpose" might be the task of creating a change and/or improving attitudes in your organization. Perhaps your aim is to increase the personal performance of your audience. Obviously, the two aims are independent, but can they be interrelated and incorporated into one media presentation?

THINK... What is the purpose of my presentation? Write it down, study it, and meditate on it.

Is the purpose of your presentation to motivate the members of your corporation to achieve a financial goal directly or indirectly? Is it your desire to challenge apathetic employees to change their behavior and actively participate in corporate efforts? Perhaps your aim is to teach new employees corporate policies and procedures and motivate them to greater work output. Do you wish to have your presentation combine updated product knowledge for the sales force and motivational materials aimed at changing old industry habits? Do you want a closing tool which brings greater financial rewards to your salesmen? Read on!

Keep the PURPOSE (AIM) simple and clear.

You must know where you are going, or you'll never know if you have arrived. Document your AIM in writing. Use the space below to document your AIM. This form of commitment will reveal the strength of your AIM. Once you have reached a decision as to the AIM, don't waver from your written goal.

☐ Promote Your Company
☐ Sell a Product
☐ Training
☐ Inspiration
☐ Public Relations: Community, Internal, etc.
☐ New Product Release
☐ Document an Event
☐ Video Memo
☐ Other

Audience

READ CAREFULLY:
This will ultimately be the most important section for creating a successful video or any presentation for that matter.

Communicating to an Audience:

Communication, according to Webster, is the "act of revealing and transmitting information from one source to another". However, "communication" implies that these ideas and concepts are received and understood, not merely viewed and discarded.

Effective communication must result in retained information by the audience. How much and how well can you communicate your purpose to your audience? Will they receive and retain what you hope to communicate? Can they, and will they, remember the most important point of your presentation?

Understanding the Mind of Your Audience:

Now that you understand that your audience has certain needs, what is the best method for them to receive information. Let us examine the mechanism by which they receive... **The Mind.**

The mind of man can be compared to a video tape recorder. The pictures and sounds we record with a video system are available to be played back when prompted by the operator. This holds true for the mind of man as well. What is seen and heard is stored in memory and is then recalled when the brain is prompted. Hence, the two systems are similar... What you see and hear is what you get. In addition to sight and sound, the human system simultaneously records other tracks like smell, touch, taste, and emotions. How does this information help in analyzing your audience? Just as an operator pushes a button on a video recorder and reviews pre-recorded pictures and audio, likewise the human mind is triggered by external stimuli (a sound, a picture, music, smell etc.) which rewinds memory tapes to a similar event in his or her memory, bringing all the emotions (feelings) of those memories to the conscious mind, setting up images (sound, sight, emotion, etc.) for reference and use. These might be referred to as *motivating memories*.

Consider information which is stored over the lifetime in the memory of an individual as either:

1. Sights, sounds and emotions that have "identifiable" meaning or value.

2. Sights, sounds and emotions that have little or no "identifiable" meaning or value.

For example: A soundtrack of a French couple calmly discussing (in French) political problems has little or no identifiable meaning to a group of English speaking first-graders from Knoxville, Tennessee. But, a picture of an ice cream cone and a soundtrack offering free ice cream cones to all first-graders would bring excitement to the young group. Images of Nazi war camps might bring painful feelings, tears, and/or anger among a Jewish group, yet cause much less of a reaction among other ethnic groups, and even denial among Anti-Semitic groups. This technique is referred to by Madison Avenue as "hidden persuaders".

The point: the use of sights and sounds with "identifiable" meaning and value cause certain actions and feelings to occur. If you understand the audiences' background (recordings), then you will use pictures and sounds that will most effectively move your audience in the direction you desire to take them. This concept is simple enough, isn't it?

Make a conscious effort to identify the *motivating memories* of your audience and to effectively and artistically portray a presentation of sights and sounds which have identifiable meaning or value to them. For example, the favorite music of baby boomers is 50's and 60's rock 'n' roll while Prime Lifer's enjoy the Big Bands and Frank Sinatra. Remember, your happy memory may be someone else's nightmare. Do your homework. Know your audience.

The Pain-Pleasure Zones of Your Audience:

Once you have a good handle on the concept of how the mind of man functions (like a video tape recorder), consider the decision and discerning area of the mind called the "pleasure-pain zone" or as some call it the "comfort zone." The "comfort zone" is a category of pictures, emotions, sounds, feelings, tastes, etc. with which the mind is familiar and accepts as its domain for existence. Once outside this domain, the mind experiences pain or discomfort, then reacts to preserve itself by motivating actions that drive the individual back into his/her comfort zone. READ THAT AGAIN!... Now what are some things, events, tastes, etc., which are in your pleasure-pain zone? How about spinach? Communists? Puppies? Hot-dogs? Catholics? Protestants? Cadillac's? Elvis? Note the comfort or pain of one person may be very different than that of another. For example, a six foot man who weighs 280 lbs. may pay little attention to the types of food he eats (fast food, etc.) while another six foot, 175 lb. man may be very health conscious and greatly aware of the effects of a high sugar and fat diet. An advertisement for doughnuts would affect the two men in very different ways. Ethnic background, present work environment (urban/rural), religious affiliation, colors, and music styles are just a few of the examples of areas where comfort (pain-pleasure) zones are a consideration.

Here is the "key":

PEOPLE DO NOT LIKE TO LEAVE THEIR COMFORT ZONE! THEY RESIST CHANGE. CHANGE IS PERCEIVED AS PAIN OR DISCOMFORT.

Even if an environment is painful, it is a "known commodity". Change may cause fear of greater discomfort and will cause the audience to resist moving. What pictures and programs has your audience stored over their lifetime? What is their comfort zone? Define their corporate pleasure-pain zone (their collective pleasure-pain zone).

As an exercise, consider the comfort zones with regard to images, color, music, desires, distaste's, etc. of the groups below. Think of regional differences (southwest vs. northeast), age differences (senior citizens vs. baby boomers), and educational differences (post graduates vs. high school dropouts).

Teenagers	**Teachers**	**Clergy**
Urban Dwellers	**Politicians**	**Mothers**
Affluent People	**Students**	**Leaders**
Farmers	**Working Class**	**Executives**
Military	**Liberal Activists**	**Kids**
Ethnic Groups	**Nuns**	**News People**
Right-to-Lifers	**Cooks**	**Sportsmen**

In the corporate world we might consider the pain-pleasure zones of corporate management, salesmen, buyers, high-tech personnel, accountants, secretaries, production personnel and end users.

Who is your Audience ?

Define Your Audience in Detail!   This is the greatest area of failure when beginning a video project. Don't assume anything. Write down an accurate profile of your audience. Ask questions!
Do research!

Now, take a few moments and describe the audience you are targeting with your video:

Define and describe your target Audience:

☐ Satisfied customer?
☐ Former customer with reservations?
☐ Not a customer, but a serious inquiry?
☐ Uninformed public?
☐ Other: write it down below:

What will motivate them to continue their loyalty? The Audience *Pleasure* zone is:

☐ Service
☐ Quality
☐ Price
☐ Other: write it down below:

What will cause them to turn to the competition? The Audience *Pain* zone is:

☐ Bad Service
☐ Poor Quality
☐ Pricing
☐ Other: write it down below:

What image (Audience perceptions) will draw new customers toward your product or service?

What will motivate your audience to participate in your program or buy your service or product?

☐ Fear of loss
☐ Religious or value conviction
☐ Be recognized as a user of your product (Mercedes)
☐ Savings
☐ Fun
☐ Hunger
☐ Peace of mind
☐ Need for your service of product

List Other perceived benefits below:

What benefits will inspire your audience to spend more time and money to further a specific cause?

What identifiable sights (pictures) will bring pleasure or pain to your audience?   Describe briefly below:

Where will your Audience view your presentation?

☐ Are they a captured audience assembled for a meeting?
☐ Are they paying?
☐ Are they an uninterested, yet potential customer?
☐ Will they view your video only once or multiple times?
☐ At work?...
☐ Home?...
☐ Public presentation?

This will help determine the length of your video and aid in developing the approach.

Have you thoroughly analyzed your audience (the working of their collective minds)? Have you defined their associated comfort zones? This approach will lay the foundation for an effective presentation with discernible impact. Answers to the aforementioned questions should be written down. It will take sensitivity, empathy, honesty, and demographic and psychographic research to answer these questions thoroughly. **The success of your project rests on your ability to meet your audience where they are while motivating them toward your desired results.**

Use the space below to list other thoughts about your **AUDIENCE** that could help achieve your **AIM**.
Now on to the **APPROACH** that will most effective to accomplish your **AIM**.

Approach

Now that you have defined your AIM (purpose for your presentation) and analyzed your AUDIENCE, it is time to develop your APPROACH. Someone once said, *"If you are going to catch fish, you have to use attractive bait or scare them into the net"*. Everyone knows a real fisherman fishes with bait (artificial or live) that is attractive or desirable to the type of fish he or she expects to catch. Yet, many of us expect to create a presentation which catches the viewer's eye and keeps his attention *without consideration of their personal tastes*. Very often the director is only concerned with his taste. If the creative director does not ask you about your audience in detail, pay close attention! This may be a warning.

This aspect of analyzing your audience requires empathy (i.e. putting yourself in their shoes). It may be difficult for some of us to think like a fish and develop a fish's taste, but if we intend to create a presentation that brings results, we must have empathy or employ the insights of those who know their tastes and habits well. Empathy means you understand how they feel; sympathy means you join them in how they feel -- do not sympathize; empathize with your audience.

Another way of catching fish is to "scare them into the net". *The fear of loss has much more motivating power than the thought of gain!* What will motivate your audience? Consider how the fear of loss is used in advertising as a great motivating force. (limited offer! only one week left! etc.).

To best develop your APPROACH you must first answer the question your AUDIENCE is going to ask:
"SWIIFM"
This will determine if you swim or sink with your audience. So what does SWIIFM mean? Turn the page.

So What's In It For Me?

What *benefits* your audience? *Do not describe the features of your company or product* but the *benefits* it offers the specific market you are targeting. Write it down below:
- ☐ We save our customers money.
- ☐ We save our customer Time.
- ☐ Provide Safety.
- ☐ Increase profits.
- ☐ Other

Developing a powerful presentation (video or otherwise) obviously begins with knowing the benefits your product or service provides relative to the competition. But, how do you creatively develop a powerful video if you have little or no experience? To a great degree you may rely on competent experienced professionals such as a creative video group. Ad agencies often work in the world of print media and do not employ the same disciplines as those in the moving visual arena. A paragraph of well-crafted copy necessary for expressing an idea can be accomplished with few if any words and a few related video cuts.

Following are a few hints that will help you clarify your APPROACH.   *Consider the various type of advertising*:

Product Advertising.
This type of advertising illuminates what the product is or what service you provide. It was the essence of the world of advertising in the late 1940s and 50s when all you had to do was simply tell your audience what you had and what it did.

Image Advertising:
An extensive period of branding or aligning your product or service with a desirable event, location, emotion, etc. This was powerful during the 1970s and part of the 1980s.

Positioning:

Today's audience is over saturated with information. Therefore, positioning is essential. It is a matter of making a connection with the audience by placing your product or service inside an unoccupied position in ones mind. The position may be first, premium, smallest, positioned with a country or city, etc. It is a mix of the three types of advertising that will bring success, but *positioning* is the most powerful technique to employ today.

The Basic Elements in a Powerful Video

Every effective presentation has three elements. You must define these and the approach will begin to emerge or develop:

1. **PROBLEM (or CHALLENGE or NEED)**
2. **SOLUTION (or OVERCOMING THE CHALLENGE)**
3. **APPEAL**

Define the PROBLEM:

What images/ideas/situations/events describe the pain zone of your potential customer-consumer?

☐World Pollution ☐Hunger ☐Shortage ☐Danger
☐Inefficiency ☐Design ☐ Poor service
☐Lack of speed ☐Too expensive ☐Image
☐Aggravating and laborious task without your product

Define the problem or challenge your target audience has **without** your product or service:

Please note the time you spend on the problem portion of your video is short. It may simply be a 10 to 30 second statement with images that stimulate the Pain Zone of your audience.

Define the SOLUTION:

This is where you emphasize the major **benefits** of your product or service to your audience. Again, do not emphasize features only. The images (visual, narration and music) will accomplish that task.   **List the solutions:**

Begin to develop the APPEAL.

What images and words best sell your product or service?

Ask your leading sales people what works for them. What photos have worked for you in the past?

What images get your audience's attention and develop desire and interest?

What color(s) best enhance your presentation? Here is a quick and simplistic review of the psychology of color:

Green:	**Money, Credibility, Life, Stability**
Blue:	**Truth, Fidelity, Most favorite-comfortable, pleasant (especially for men)**
Red:	**Motivating, Irritating at times, Sensual**
Orange:	**Most disliked by adults-loved by kids under 4**
Purple:	**Royal, elite, important, most creativity**
Turquoise:	**Denotes discriminating taste**
Yellow:	**Happy, Growth, Home, Friendship**
Pink:	**Femininity, Motherhood, Health**

What type of music will keep them right in the center of their comfort zone? And Irritate them?

What music will make your audience feel comfortable, uneasy, repulsed, invigorated, motivated?

☐ country
☐ classical
☐ alternative
☐ 50's
☐ adult contemporary
☐ rock
☐ rap
☐ opera

What technique will best grasp and hold your audience's attention?

☐ humor
☐ statistics
☐ hi-tech
☐ educational
☐ highly recognizable spokesperson
☐ drama
☐ news
☐ story telling
☐ facts about the industry

List Others below:

What will affirm or change their feelings?

Why will they want to change, improve, and/or achieve greater heights with your product or service?

☐ The service is new and improved
☐ The product is the most competitive
☐ Your service is second to none

List Others below:

The Motive	**Possible Approach**
The need to belong-	I will lose out without you
The desire to see progress-	Certain traditions may be hindrances.
The fear of loss-in	You'll only have this offer once a lifetime...
The thought of changing-	Look what successful people do!
The desire to be like others-	Clothes make the man!
The love of country-	Our love of country is rooted in our freedoms!
The desire to make money-	Look what success buys you!
The desire to lose weight-	You can never be too thin or too rich!

Make a list of other motives and possible approaches that relate to your project in the space below.

The Motive	Possible Approach

With the previously defined information, you can now begin to work with the creative team. Develop an effective APPROACH with words, music, and visuals that will get your audience's attention. Develop an interest and produce a desire for your product or service.

Now for the fourth essential and most important step to ensure the production of a Powerful Video Presentation:

Action

"Let not your studies lead only to knowledge...
Let your studies lead to action."
William E. Bailey

If your presentation does not provoke your audience into
Action, you have missed the mark! Your message should
bring results, and that will be, as previously stated, a
"change," an "improvement," or an "achievement" in someone
or of something. Again, your presentation must **motivate
people to Action**... and that action will bring results.

What type of action do you expect your video to accomplish?

☐ **Better trained employees.**
☐ **An increase in sales production.**
☐ **A foot in the door of very large accounts.**
☐ **A new type of business from old customers.**
☐ **Increased investment from your stockholders.**
☐ **Motivated employees - improved self-esteem.**
☐ **Consumer motivated to pick up their phone.**
  and call you.
☐ **Reach a new niche market.**

Define your action in the space below:

One last point: In the realm of a diversified corporate media plan, it is sometimes difficult to determine the success of a presentation in terms of money. Financial return-on-effort may be impossible to directly gauge, especially when the consideration and purpose of your media is motivation or public relations. Nevertheless, you will see **Action** if your presentation is effective.

Once you have discussed and defined the four A's
(**AIM, AUDIENCE, APPROACH,** and **ACTION**),
you will be well on your way to producing a
powerful video. Stay tuned!!!

Notes:
Use this book for a more than knowledge... put it to action.

Notes:

Everything you want has a price connected to it. There's a price to pay if you want to make things better, a price to pay just for leaving things as they are, a price for everything.

Harry Browne

The B's of Pre-Production
Every Great Presentation
Contains these Elements

The B's of Pre-Production

Video, like any other communication medium, can be good and/or bad. David Ogilvie, one of the all time advertising genius', wrote in his book Advertising by David Ogilvie that one ad will draw 25 times more response than another. Although they are selling the same product, the ad sizes are identical and placed in equally effective locations in the same issue of a magazine, one ad will prove to be better. The ad that draws a greater response is not only creative but exercises the basics of good advertising. The same holds true for video presentations.

A video has to be more than a piece of visual and aural artistry. It must also be pragmatic. A video presentation must accomplish its AIM and move the audience to an appropriate ACTION. In the previous section the initial planning stages which include the four A's: AIM, AUDIENCE, APPROACH, and ACTION were elaborated. Have you taken the time to define and write these down? If not, stop reading now! Go back and write down your AIM, AUDIENCE, APPROACH and ACTION. Once you have the A's well defined, move on to the development of the actual flow and script of the video with help from the B's of video production:

Big Picture
Basic Solution
Become Involved

Big Picture

Create a "**Big Picture**" with your presentation. This may include one of the following categories:

1. Illumination of a PROBLEM.

In the corporate world you may encounter quality problems. This can best be illustrated in the automotive industry. America lost a significant amount of market share to the Japanese and European auto makers. In the recent past, the list of the five top quality cars in the world did not include an American car. Through meeting the needs of the consumer and mass media campaigns promoting "American Pride", "American Made", and "Jobs for Americans", the US car market is on the rise, and foreign companies are moving manufacturing to the US and hiring US auto workers. Patriotic media blitzes would not have won the battle to sell more US made vehicles if quality had not risen and prices decreased. Creatively and effectively illuminating problems and communicating real solutions is often the video producer's goal. Societal problems, such as drugs, the homeless, abortion rights, and the abused are brought to light through the video medium and the results or efforts to help are enhanced or diminished by the diligence and expertise of the presentation or producer.

2. Develop a CONFLICT.

Top films use tension to add interest: good against bad, right against wrong, God against the Devil, a "love" triangle. In industry, the conflict may be caused by diametrically opposing parameters (management vs. union workers). A case in point might be the size of a car versus gas mileage. What conflict applies in your arena?

3. Communicate a CHALLENGE.

So many times we hear about America's decline in excellence. This may be industry's greatest challenge. Research and development, education, meeting schedules, and a return to integrity in business ethics are but a few of the challenges to communicate. Overcome a moral crisis.

4. Define a DREAM or VISION

Sharing a vision to create a better product, service or a better world might be your "big picture". Use your imagination and develop a dream or vision that is uniquely your own. Back your presentation with research that will present a credible and believable way to achieve "the challenge of a life time".

5. Search for a STANDARD

Excellence, quality, and the establishment of a standard might be your
big picture. It is an important issue that may include new and innovative systems such as the safety standards recently introduced, and now commonplace, in the use of airbags for cars. A history of success that inspires teams like Alabama and Notre Dame to continue the winning tradition may become the big picture of your video presentation. Better still, perhaps your standard will challenge politicians to become statesmen.

**The "Big Picture" moves your audience
off center and grabs their attention.
Once you have the "Big Picture"
in mind, you must resolve it
with the Basic Solution.**

Notes:
Define the Challenge or Problem you will be solving
with your product or service.

Basic Solution

In a presentation, which should be positive and result in good feelings, it is important to spend only a brief time establishing the problem. This is especially true when the audience is not captive, that is, they have not paid to see the video or were not asked by their employer to attend its viewing. Here are some simple, yet effective, solutions to the BIG PICTURE.

1. We have to SOLVE the PROBLEM

Problem: mice in the rice. Here is the solution; a better mouse trap, a less expensive "gadget" that is rodent friendly (the trap does not kill the mouse). State how your goal can be accomplished and can put an end to a "pesty" and destructive problem.

2. RESOLVE the CONFLICT

Conflict: a large car with low gas mileage. Solution: reduce the weight without affecting the size and safety. Tell the secret of how it is accomplished. Conflict: A marriage is in jeopardy. Resolved: through counseling the union is repaired by revealing a breakdown in communications and expounding on the proper communication techniques. Good wins out, etc..

3. MEET the CHALLENGE

"Ask not what your country can do for you... Ask what you can do for your country". These words by John Kennedy challenged an entire generation. Challenge the audience toward tenacity, determination, hard work (the old fashion way), dedication, knowledge, leadership, inspiration, on-going education, spiritual growth, etc.. in order to achieve the Big Picture.

4. ACCOMPLISH the GOAL/VISION

For example: you might illustrate accomplishment as follows: "Finally, after 40 years, we have done it!" "For generations we have held fast to our forefather's vision and we all have a lot to thank them for". Consider the stirring words of Martin Luther King, Jr., "I have a Dream"... "We shall over come someday". Now, illustrate the stepping stones to accomplish the vision to be reached.

5. SET the STANDARD

Once the challenge is set, show the new standard of excellence achieved: new boundaries pioneered, the best of the show, the breaking of an Olympic record, the discovery of new non-invasive medical treatments, the return of factual journalism. These are a few ideas which illustrate the need for you to define a Basic Solution for the Big Picture. Do not under-estimate the power of simplicity.
Keep it simple and be sure you execute the basics described above. You will find it is more important to accomplish the client's goals than win awards from your peers in the advertising community.

Notes:
What is the Basic Solution to your presentation challenge?

Become Involved

Once you have defined your **BIG PICTURE** and **BASIC SOLUTION**, keep in mind that the ultimate goal is to get people to **BECOME INVOLVED**.

When all is said and done, you must ask yourself, will this video motivate the audience. Will there be an emotional connection made?

Buy Your Products?
Contribute to your charity?
Use Your Service?
Change their Opinion about Your Products?
Send Money?
Vote Yes?
Attend Your Facility?
Participate in Your Cause?
Develop an Interest in this New Method?
Choose Your Resort and Visit?
Work Harder at their Job?
Become a Partner Instead of Just a Worker?
Continue to Believe You Offer the Best Service?
Travel on your airline?
Buy season passes?
Call Your Company for a Free...?

The **BIG PICTURE** should be "attention getting" (move your audience off center) and produce interest while the **BASIC SOLUTION** should motivate and convince your audience to **BECOME INVOLVED**. Techniques utilized to accomplish these tasks vary. The use of audio visual images drive the audience out of their comfort zone by use of shock, excitement, hate, joy, horror, failure, injustice, beauty, and so on. Offering a logical, humane, right, or correct solution or path of resolve, aids in their involvement or choice of action.

How do you appeal to your audience to become involved. What Action do you expect them to take once they viewed your presentation?

With these principles in mind, proceed with the conceptualizing and writing of a script.

Review your A's (**AIM, AUDIENCE, APPROACH, & ACTION**). Make a list of the B's (**BIG PICTURE, BASIC SO-LUTION, & BECOME INVOLVED**) that best serve your presentation needs. Once you are convinced you will accomplish the task at hand with the A's and B's, move on to the C's of successful video production.

Knowing where you are going is all you need to get there.

Carl Frederick

The C's of Pre-Production
Three Necessary Steps for Success

The C's of Pre-Production

You have almost completed the all-important "Win Before You Begin" phase of producing a successful presentation. The A's and B's are seeds that are planted and germinated in the creative process. Birthing the C's comes in production.

Just how important is this section? Raiders of the Lost Ark is the perfect example of how important the C's of production are to success. The screenwriter engaged in a collaborative effort with George Lucas and Steven Spielberg
to produce one of Hollywood's top grossing films. As the story goes, the three creative minds wrote the final script after discussing what events they always wanted to see in a adventure movie. "Snakes, thousands of snakes" and "a great big ball chasing the hero", were two of the scenes which were written, critiqued, and rewritten into one of the most exciting movies of all time. The process: concepts to script, critique, production of the rewritten script. By the way, there are no great script writers; only Re-writers.

A good script can make a director, but even a great director can not always produce a good movie with a bad script. It begins with the conceptual flow. It is my belief that this phase, the **ABC's, is the most important phase in the video creation process**. Pay close attention to the art and science of the following steps:

Conceptual Flow
Composing a Script
Critique

Conceptual Flow

Create a Conceptual Flow: A conceptual flow, or outline, is a sequential list of events that occur in the video presentation. This includes a description of all the topics and visuals of the video as they appear in order. Always have all key decision makers (video producer, creative director and company executives) agree on the conceptual flow and have it signed off before you create a script (signatures of all decision makers should be obtained before you begin script writing). You may have copies of the schedule and responsibilities for tasks to be accomplished also attached for signing. If your client is responsible for talent
releases, permits, and other important items, attach that agreement and have it signed off before proceeding to assure there is no misunderstandings as to what all players must do to accomplish a tight schedule and stay on budget. The more details of the video production you have defined and signed off, the more successful you will be as a producer. Do not proceed without a clear documented agreement of all details by all the decision makers. Surprises are almost always costly and even damaging to the final outcome of your project.

Now you are ready to proceed in the development of your Conceptual Flow, the first "C" of a successful presentation:

Give Your Audience the Unexpected.
Remember, the mind will develop "perceptual filters" to block out familiar and commonplace information and images. So, give your audience the unexpected! Someday the unusual will become commonplace, then you can use
what used to be commonplace as the unusual (Woodstock then and now). Getting and keeping the attention of your audience to achieve your purpose will require that you surprise, shock, or somehow move your audience with the unexpected. Even when educating, you must peak interest with the unexpected.

Take Your Audience Out of Their Environment.
Most people, unfortunately, are not content with their lives. Taking people forward in time (Star Wars, Back to the Future) or back in time (Chariots of Fire, Howard's End, etc.) has proven to be a very successful money making technique. It is a well-known secret that man will more readily receive from a stranger ("a prophet is without honor in his own town"), than he will from friends and family. Do not take this concept lightly when conceptualizing your presentation. Disarm the viewer with a new world/new environment: a majestic scene in the South Seas, cardboard shelters of the homeless.

Contradict a Well-known or accepted Truth.
"I will prove there is no God." To a church audience, this would be an alarming contradiction of the truth. "On a clear day, you can see Hawaii from Los Angeles. Here, look how close they are on the map... only 3 inches away." Sometimes a contradiction will get attention and move your audience. To be effective, you must be sure your contradiction is obvious to all.

You Can Say That Again... You Can Say That Again.
The secret to "Madison Avenue advertising" is repetition. Not only does a detergent commercial come into your home 40 or 50 times a day, but in each repetition of the ad you are first told (sold): what they are going to do. Next,
they do it; and at last, they tell you what they've just done. Many other products use this time-proven formula. Repeat your point in many ways and forms throughout the presentation. Utilize lyrics, pictures, illustrations, testimonies, and narration to say it... and say it again.

Make One Point:
I have a poster in my office which says: "The main thing is to keep the main thing the main thing". If your audience remembers one thing, "the main thing", (your main point) you are on your way to success! So, repeat your "purpose" many times in many ways. Do not present more than your audience

can absorb or easily remember. Most of the time a short presentation is more effective than a long presentation. For example, a three to five minute presentation is an acceptable length for a promotional presentation. Fifteen minutes and beyond is acceptable for a teaching presentation, but in most cases, is too long for a promotional. Too often the client wants to "say it all" when most often the goal is to sell a product or service and not to thoroughly educate. Entertainment media can be much longer (1 hour plus) in that concentrated thought or memorization is not a requirement.

Never Admit You Are Presenting An Educational or Sales Presentation.

The purpose of your presentation may be educational or sales oriented, but the means of reaching that destination can be greatly enhanced by an entertaining format. For example, a presentation for children's education might be narrated by a child and filled with music ("Hooked on Phonics worked for me!"). By entertaining your audience, the lesson is caught, rather than directly taught. It is a good rule to evaluate your presentation on entertainment value first, then be sure the presentation meets its purposes. Keep their interest!

Presenting something "different" is the key to getting attention and developing interest.

The first basic step to selling is getting attention. The second is developing interest. The five steps to selling should be considered when conceptualizing a script: 1. attention, 2. interest, 3. desire, 4. close, 5. fulfill the promise/follow-up. Television programs and commercials do the craziest things imaginable to achieve "the sale". They must get your attention in a mega-media world. List some conceptual approaches you think will be "different" and grab the attention of your audience. Choose different approaches that may be emotional, humorous, high action, or mysterious.

One other thing to consider: what level of awareness does the product or service have with your target audience? Product awareness falls into three general categories and requires three different approaches:

1. Pioneering Effort: Your audience must be taught what your product is, what it does, and how your product benefits them. A typical example might be new hi-tech items such as the computer scanner, software programs, personal communications systems, etc..

2. Competitive Effort: Your product use and benefits are well understood, but a number of companies offer virtually the same form and function. Soap, food, clothes, hair products, mouse traps, etc.. In this case, the creative challenge is to show your product in a different light or develop associations that cause the audience to perceive they will receive additional benefits when using the product.

3. Keep Alive: Your product is the leader in your industry. Your goal is to maintain your share of the market and not lose ground; Coke, Chevy, etc.. Consider the position of your product or service in the marketplace when creating the conceptual flow of your presentation. It helps to test your ideas and concepts on a target market. Again, there are specialized companies that do "test marketing". Utilize such a service when the stakes are high, such as an expensive national advertising campaign. However, it is important to test your ideas, even on a small scale. Find out if your video draws the calculated or desired response through test marketing to a small segment of your target market before distributing to the masses.

The creative process of developing a conceptual flow, as well as writing a script, includes the following ingredients:
ILLUMINATION...
INSPIRATION...
INCUBATION...
ACTIVATION.

Illumination:
Collect facts. Read all brochures, literature, advertising and public relations materials available from your client. Study the industry/product, the competition, demographics, geographics, psychographics, and the newly added spirographics (spiritual values as they relate to your project). Use the library liberally. Next, be sure to spend quality time with your client absorbing his or her ideas, tastes, and style. Your client must feel good about what you create as it represents him and/or his product to his market. Make sure you have the input of all the decision makers. The facts with which you illuminate your mind will be used to create the presentation and produce an effective communications tool. Remember, it is essential that your client is comfortable with the presentation. It to his desired action.

Inspiration:
Ideas and concepts are formed. What unusual approach will you take? What comfortable words will soothe your audience? What will shock them? Write them down on the back of this page. Don't think you will remember all of the ideas that come to mind. Write down words and visual concepts. They are easily forgotten when you are working on several projects at one time. Do not make light of how easily inspiration may come to mind. Most often, it is the inspired idea that just "drops out of the sky" that makes the difference between a hit and a mediocre presentation.

Incubation:
Rushing the creative process can rob you of the best. Digest and think over your concepts and facts. This is a must! Plan on taking time to incubate the concepts you have in mind surrounded by a relaxed or stimulating setting (the beach... inspiring music, etc.). Out of incubation will come additional inspiration and new concepts and development.

Activation:
Once you have developed your conceptual flow, share your ideas with your client or sponsor. You must remember, how you look does not depend on what you wear, but how you feel about what you wear. What form of dress do you prefer: formal wear or jeans? Soft unstructured dressing or tailored classics? Subtle neutrals or bold patterns and colors? Your sponsor/client must feel comfortable with your concepts. The client's comfort with the end product is always more important than yours. They have to fit his style and comfort zone. This might take some salesmanship and compromise. If the client's comfort zone cramps your style or you believe his changes will harm the final project, review the A's and B's with him to clarify your approach. After the client agrees to the flow and plan of action for the project, make all required changes and additions in your conceptual flow and document it. Then, have them sign your contract or agreement. At this point in production, you should have required and received at least one third to one half of the payment for the total project.

How to develop a Conceptual Flow or outline on paper.
The conceptual flow may include five to ten general segments for an entire video. For example, a travel video might be broken into the following
segments:
1. Intro: Hot, upbeat music and pictures of well known travel sights.
2. Big Picture: The conflict: The travel industry is changing. Beware if you are deciding to start a travel agency.
3. Basic Solution: Experts say successful agencies execute the following....
4. The ABC Travel Network offers new agencies the following to assure their success in the travel business.
5. Appeal to Action (Become Involved) The travel business can be fun and profitable. Testimonies by successful members of the ABC Travel Network who reaffirm the specific points made about what successful agencies do and how ABC helped them excel.

6. Close with excitement: Travel sights, cruises, etc.. Be sure to include the theme of adventure, fun, excitement, and prosperity that the prospective client can expect to experience in the travel business.

Keep in mind your A's and B's and create a presentation with impact and information.

Once you have a Conceptual Flow on paper, share it with your client. This will take explanation. Most clients will have to be sold on the ideas presented. Be open to ideas and possible misunderstandings that may have developed and adjust the conceptual flow accordingly. After having sat through hours of meetings, I have proceeded to create a conceptual flow, only to realize upon presentation, that my ideas were counter-productive to those of personnel who were not in the initial meeting. Once the conceptual flow is agreed upon, print a copy of the final flow for each of the key decision makers. Leave enough space (lines) at the bottom for the signatures of each involved party beginning with your name. Have a date next to each name. This will help to move the project along and short-circuit any delays. Now you are ready to write the script. List the five to ten general segments to be presented in your video (conceptual flow) below and on the back of this page.

Composing a Script

Script writing for visual media is quite different than ad, print or book writing. You have to develop the discipline of writing with pictures or film in mind. Put your feet in the shoes of the audience and see what they see. It has been said a picture is worth a thousand words. There are cases when words will never convey the emotion you can provoke with a picture. One example is the award winning photo of *The Sudan Girl*. This photograph was taken by Kevin Carter in 1994. It illustrates a starving child, dying from malnutrition and a lack of medical attention as she attempts to crawl to a United Nations food station. A buzzard perches behind her waiting for her to die so he can eat. You can view it at http://sites.psu.edu/blogforrcl/2012/10/17/the-worst-kind-of-suffering/ Any words I might pen would never move an audience like this photo. For those who take the time to view this heart moving photo you should know she made it to her destination. A friend of mine knows the Carter family and they explained that Kevin saw her to her destination. One picture or film clip series will convey so much more than words. So...

Let pictures help write the script!

Example:

Video Theme: Financial Services

Film Collage: a series of pictures including a Wall Street sign, the Stock Market Exchange, crowds of business people time lapse high speed, cars on the move, etc.

Script: Financial Services; a 33 Trillion dollar market.

Notes:
List a few pictures that communicated what you are trying to say to your audience with as few words as you are able to tell your story.

A script for a simple 30 second commercial might be done on a napkin while sipping coffee. The other side of script composition can be found in a feature length screen play. There are a number of software programs such as **Final Draft** which is popular for the Hollywood script. In fact you must follow this format to even get your script read by the studios. There are a few exception like you're married to George Lucas. If you are doing a screen play use Final Draft which interplays with Movie Magic Scheduler and Budgeting software. These are a must for producing a film.

Before you purchase **Final Draft,** Celtx found at www.celtx.com is a software program that has some great features for a number of different types of script writing projects. The project templates available in this free software include:
Film
Audio Visual
Theatre
Audio Play
Storyboard
Comic Book
Novel

Download Celtx and get familiar with the film writing format. There are only a few styles (categories) to learn:

Scene Heading	Ctrl 1
Action	Ctrl 2
Character	Ctrl 3
Dialog	Ctrl 4
Parenthetical	Ctrl 5
Transition	Ctrl 6
Shot	Ctrl 7
Text	Ctrl 8

Final Draft is the movie standard but check for new software from time to time. You will love the ease with which you will write professional scripts using these well produced, easy-to-use software programs.

Critique

Evaluation of Your Presentation

The success and impact of your presentation will strongly depend on your ability to evaluate your work. Evaluation is not an opinion or subjective view offered by the man on the street. It is a measurement of your presentation by guidelines or standards. One might call it a judgment of the effectiveness in creatively meeting your objectives and purposes. Start in the design phase and evaluate concepts in relationship to your audience. Secondly, be sure to ask qualified or informed people the right questions about the script. "Evaluate the evaluator and do not believe everything you hear." Remember, everyone has opinions. Go outside your creative team whenever possible for objectivity. Do not be a defensive producer who argues with any criticism, but readily accept input from qualified people. Be honest and willing to change, redo, and recreate where necessary. Hard work and proper evaluation at each step will prove to be worth its weight in gold.

"DON'T CRITICIZE, CRITIQUE"

I believe Walt Disney's great success was partially achieved by the fact that he never allowed criticism of ideas, no matter how ridiculous they might have seemed at the time. Those crazy ideas might have use in the next project. Critique the validity of an idea for your production or script, but don't criticize the person or group who dares to express (his/their) creativity.

CRITIQUE YOUR SCRIPT

Here are a number of points you can use to critique your script.

Title: Will it grab the audience's attention?
Is it appropriate for the Aim?
Is there high identity in the title?

Lead:
Are the first words an interest grabber?
Is it well-established for your topic?

Organization:
Is there a clear focus on your approach?
Is the central purpose of your video stated?
Are the main points logically and effectively presented?

Content:
Are the ideas well developed?
Are the illustrations and details clear and applicable? Does the script have originality?

Style:
Is the copy interesting and varied?
Is the vocabulary appropriate or beyond/below the audience? Does the music compliment the narrator and express the desired emotion?

Documentation:
Is the research evident or is the script shallow?
Are the sources credible and current?

Development of Ideas:
Are the thoughts thoroughly developed?
Are there any unfinished ideas?

Conclusion:
Will the audience be absolutely involved?
Will your aim and goal be achieved?

Movement:
Is there a logical flow (continuity)?
Are there good transitions?

Notes:
Once your script or screen play is written critique it with these
topics in mind.

Nothing is particularly hard if you divide them into small jobs.

Henry Ford

5

Production Steps to Success
The Basic Flow and Steps of Producing a Video

Basic Flow for Producing a Video

Producing a video can be as simple as using one camera to document a speech ore event or it may be a million dollar project which includes hundreds of people and thousands of man hours of production. No matter what the complexity, producing a video includes, but is not limited to, the following phases:

1. **PRE-PRODUCTION (PLANNING)**

Creative Session:	Go over chapters 1 and 2
Research:	Polls. competition, image, etc.
Conceptual Flow:	Signed-off by the client
Script & Storyboard:	Storyboard in writing.

(Illustrated storyboards are provided for most high-end agency work)

Final Edited Script:	Signed-off by the client
Casting and Legal:	Release forms
Schedule:	Shoot Log, Dates, etc.

2. **PRODUCTION**

Assembly of Resources:	
Fabrication:	Props, Sets, Costumes, etc.
Video Shoots:	Location, Studio
Music:	Creation or Selection
Narration:	Audio Studio
Paper Edit:	If necessary, from window dubs

3. **POST PRODUCTION**

Custom Video Graphics
Editing
Packaging
Review
Master Final Edited Copy—File
Video Duplication or Presentation

Here are a few subtopics which may be added to planning, production, and postproduction (renting equipment, design of video jacket and labels, the creation of custom music and sound effects, special illustrations for custom titles and graphics, dollies or a steady-cam, etc.). The above topics expand to meet the complexity of the presentation.

Pre-Production
(Planning Approval Stages)

Once you have picked the best production company for your task (see Chapter 6—next) and have given them the appropriate deposit then you are ready to begin.

Creative Session

After your initial meeting the **AIM** should be well defined. Your **AUDIENCE** should be profiled with definite clarity, and the **APPROACH** should be discussed to offer the most effective impact on your audience.   A CREATIVE SESSION will produce ideas that bring your theme to life. By the way I must state that I have been often surprised at how even a CFO will come up with brilliant ideas if everyone is allowed to just flow without no's and never interjected. Video production is a collaborative activity.

Research

Base your discussion on well founded research. David Ogilvy is considered by many the father of modern advertizing. His campaigns have lasted for decades. "Don't Leave Home Without It" the tag line for American Express Traveler's Cheques is one of many of his award winning campaigns. He attributes his success to his initial years of work with Gallop. Research is important. One of the most successful campaigns I produced for a hi-tech company which lasted for over twenty years and produced millions of dollars in sales for my client started with research. We called our potential customers and let them tell us what they needed and how to approach the task.

Conceptual Flow

Out of these creative efforts should emerge a CONCEPTUAL FLOW or outline.. The conceptual flow should cover the **Basics Elements for a Powerful Video** (pages 29 and 30). Your approval of these factors should be acknowledged in writing, and indicate that all parties clearly understand the expectations of the undertaking at hand.

Script & Scripted Story Board

The next step is to translate the conceptual flow into a script. The script is the most important element in the process; a good script well give birth to a successful video while a poor or even bad script utilizing the best Hollywood actors will result in a bomb. Along with the script should be a "Scripted Story Board" which is a written description of the visuals located to the right of the script (not drawings). Here is a simple sample with a narrator as the only talent. When other spokes persons are involve another column to the left of the script is required:

IMAGE ARTISTRY FILM & VIDEO

Client: Q82
Project: Reverse Mortgage
Working Title: Equity in Your Home Put to Good Use
Date: Feb 7, 2014
Producer: Jim Beach
Director: Domenic Fusco

#	V/O - MUSIC	VISUALS
01	So many Americans work their entire lives only to find they aren't able to enjoy the rich and rewarding retirement they envisioned. (do all that they envisioned).	Visuals of industry, city life, people in a hurry, etc.
		Washington DC Homes of a variety of values
	Now, a government backed reverse mortgage will allow you to simply unlock the money sitting in your home for anything you desire. Pay off your present mortgage, take a long overdue vacation, help the grand kids with tuition, reduce medical bills. Anything!	Vacation shots grand kids medical bills
	Here are a few important facts about a reverse mortgage;.	(Character generation in blue) Facts about a Reverse Mortgage
	• It allows homeowners, at least 62 years of age, to access equity in their home. The money you receive is tax-free and can be used for any purpose.	At least 62 years of age
		The Money is Tax Free No Restrictions on Use
	• You always retain ownership of your home and may live on the property for as long as you choose – without ever making a mortgage payment.	You Retain Ownership
	• In fact, repayment isn't required until the home is no longer your primary residence. All you do is	

This is the most critical aspect of the video project since all production and post production are completely dependent on the video script. The client should be *absolutely sure* the script does exactly what he or she wants it to produce before proceeding. Changing one's mind later is costly in every sense.

Once all principals have agreed on the script, acknowledge your approval in writing. You have accomplished the most important aspect of producing an effective and powerful video. So, an acknowledgment in writing means serious business. It also signifies that any future changes in the script means a change in the negotiated price of the project.

Casting

One of the most important lessons I have acquired over the years as a director is to hire the best talent available suited of the task and under direct. This holds true for voice-over talent. I once hired a CNN news caster for a project and had to redo his work. We found the audience listening to his voice, that is *how* he was "saying" and not *what* he was saying. Great "readers" are rare. They connect with the audience by acting with their voice resulting in the audience intently listening what he or she is "saying".

Another generalization I have gleaned from years of producing and directing is on camera talent can be dangerous for the task. Especially when using known actors. Men and women tend to look at the talent and judge their look, clothing, etc. A sure thing is to use visuals to communicate the script and where possible stay away from talent unless they are testimonies or a word from the president/CEO. Just a thought. All generalizations are false including this one.

Legal

Be sure to have all your talent sign a *talent release form*. I have never had a legal problem after producing over 900 projects. But stick to the basics and show your client the professional side of your business.

Production Scheduling

A production schedule should be created, even if it is a very simple list of shooting dates and a tentative video due date. Often clients do not schedule well or prepare ahead and the production company must change shooting schedules. Such changes, particularly short notice changes, have a considerable impact on finances and meeting the production schedule. Realize the impact and the cost of changes.

Notes:

whoever wishes to become great among you
shall be your servant.

Bible Mark 10:43

How to Choose the
Best Production Company

What to Look For and
the Right Questions to Ask

What to Look For...
The Right Questions To Ask!

Don't Believe Everything You Hear

Look at their work and be critical.
Do you like their work? Does it have impact?
Is it informative? Is it up-to-date?
Look at their work and be critical.
Do you believe they are able to create the content and image you require? Can they meet your objectives?
Look at their work and be critical.
*Make sure the demo you view represents the real work of the crew who will produce for you. If you have any doubts **check references**!!!*

Follow your own feelings about **the impact, believability** and **communication strength** concerning the video production company's products, key personnel and ability to serve you. Be sure to utilize the information in this book in order to approach your project with the basic knowledge of what a successful video project contains. Remember, producer/ directors are like artists. Some utilize animation, some fine art, while others create with humor or drama. Find a comfortable fit. There are creative directors who can knock you off your seat with artistic "bells and whistles" and yet they may entirely miscommunications the facts necessary to move your audience to act. Likewise, a programmatic approach without market friendly images and flair may bore your audience. Do your research! Look, listen and feel the work of the production company you are considering.

DO NOT always judge by price. Decide what type of video you **must** have to meet your minimum requirements, then choose a producer who will easily meet your minimum standard. Choose a production group that possesses the necessary talent to achieve your desired results. **Beware of the agency who finds it necessary to shoot 20 hours of footage from which**

they expect to choose only five minutes. Although this might be applicable when producing a documentary, it might be inexperience or an excuse to extend your budget. Know where you are going in order to save time and money; and at the same time, produce a more effective video. A "**You Win Before You Begin**" approach works better than the hit and miss method.

A good video must contain information which directly relates to your audience. This information is gathered from research directly from you. The task of the producer and writer is to technically and artistically put this information into a visually attractive form while achieving the predetermined goals. In other words, it is a team effort. Beware of the creative team that does not look to you for research data, product knowledge, and your expert sales experience.

What to Expect from a Producer

Will the producer/director maintain the proper corporate image and integrity?

Your "image" is what people imagine you are, and what people imagine you do! You project an image (whether you are conscious of it or not), and that image is implanted in the mind of the beholder. That mental picture is a descriptive story of who you are and what you do. It may not be a "true" story of who you are and what you do, but it is projected immediately to your viewing audience. Make sure the integrity of your product and corporate image is defined clearly to the creative team in the initial planning and creative sessions.

"Your IMAGE is more important than REALITY because your IMAGE is REALITY to the observer."

Your image immediately creates a feeling and belief system in the mind of the observer. What the observer sees and hears in your video presentation stimulates the brain to pull images (thoughts) from memory which create a composite picture of who the observer believes you are. These images create feelings about you. There are three basic dimensions to the image you create with video:

Visual Image

The pictures that flash by, the product packaging, and the people that appear on the screen (their hair, clothes, facial expression, body language, age, male or female, eyes, teeth, smile, ethnic mix, the actual set, its style, colors, etc....) stimulate the viewers to think about what those images represent and mean to them. This will produce the result as discussed in chapter 3.0.

Audio Image

How the narrator speaks, the tone of his or her voice, the descriptive phrases, the attitude of delivery (negative, positive, strong, critical, nice, harsh, confident, secure, insecure, insincere, patronizing, nurturing, humorous or serious, etc.) is as important as the visual image. In fact, George Lucas believes that the "sound is half of the picture". Music is also more important than you might imagine. While only 5% to 10% of what is spoken is recalled, music (jazz, rock, reggae, classical, new age, rap, opera, easy listening) creates an indelible impression that represents who you are to your audience. The choice of a melody and style—instrumental or vocal— projects feelings that will stay with the listener long after your video ends. A successful jingle may be remembered for decades after the visual from whence it came is totally forgotten. Match your choice with your demographics. Match your choice with your message and image.

Emotional Image

The composite of your presentation (industrious, honest, motivated, exciting, innovative, sensual, caring, futuristic, neurotic, established, spiritual) will convey an emotional image. Hopefully, you have pre-designed your presentation to accomplish your AIM and ACTION. As you develop your script, select your spokesperson, score your music themes, and choose your scenic properties, make sure they consistently present an image that delivers emotional impact—the emotional impact you desire. Don't send MIXED messages.

The image you emote will create feelings of credibility, desire, trust, etc. (or lack of each). The feelings you create will determine your future success or possible failure. **Image** is what people "think you are".

Can and will the producer maintain or strengthen your corporate image? The "power of image" is often not calculated. Good images are like tickets. If you have the ticket you get into the game. Consider how many salespeople never reach the decision makers who might purchase their wares because a receptionist does not like the way he or she looks and/or what he or she projects. **First impressions are lasting ones! It is difficult to recreate a public image gone awry.** Consider: Dan Quayle, Richard Nixon, Tonya Harding and O.J. Simpson.

Consider Your Corporate Image (part of your branding):
Will the image of the video convey what you are and/or what you want to be? Is it COHESIVE? That is, is the final product logically consistent with your printed materials? Will all the media you produce convey what you wish to express? You may ask "Why develop a cohesive image?" First and foremost, it costs money—lots of money—every time you change your image. Corporate communiqué's should carry a consistent image. This will enforce and reinforce an impression you wish to imprint on the minds of your customers and potential customers efficiently. Every piece of media that presents a different image means you are re-educating the buyer. Assume your present image is working. If you are looking for change or to define your new product, services or goals, **be deliberate about choosing an image.** Be sure to maintain that image that works for you in the market place. (i.e. "Coke is It!") Remember, your image is "who you *really* are" in the mind of the viewer.

In summary, know what you want to accomplish. Select a co-operative and creative production team in whom you have confidence. Now you are on your way to experiencing the exciting and rewarding process of producing a powerful video presentation!

Notes:

Everybody has to be somebody to somebody to be anybody.

Malcolm S. Forbes

No One Person is a Team
Your Contribution to a Successful Video

Your Contribution to a Successful Video Project

How to support the video production team.

Once you have chosen your production company, be sure to diligently support the project. This can be accomplished through the following:

1. Stay on top of details!

Assist in the collection of the project materials which are called for in the script. Make all printed materials on your company, product, staff or concept available to the production team from the beginning. Also, make archival materials available (historical documents, laboratory or research reports, photo files, newsworthy clippings or video coverage, etc...).

Make a list of resources needed for the project and critical success factors such as key personnel, products and events that must be documented for the project.

_____

_____

_____

_____

_____

_____

_____

_____

_____

_____

_____

_____

_____

2. Do not change the schedule unless it is absolutely necessary!

Unless death, illness, or disaster strikes, keep APPOINTMENTS! Time is money. Jot down the important deadlines and keep in mind vacation time for the decision makers:

A. PLANNING

Concepts Meeting: _____

Research: _____

Conceptual Flow: _____

Script & Storyboard: _____

B. PRODUCTION

Assembly of Resources: _____

Fabrication: _____

Video Shoots: _____

_____

_____

_____

Narration: _____

C. POST PRODUCTION

Editing _____

Packaging _____

Review _____

Master Final _____

Video Duplication _____

Presentation Date: _____

3. Let the talent do their work.

It is rare to have a corporate executive try to direct a shoot, but there are those "frustrated artists" who criticize or scrutinize every detail and find it necessary to interject mandatory "suggestions". Artistic choice must be entrusted to your producer/director. Unless the visuals are a detriment or inferior, allow the producer/director to execute the job he or she has been paid to do after the script is signed off. Your input should be heavy during preproduction and scripting and reduced to oversight during shooting and editing.

Make a list of key personnel in your corporation that will assist the video production company in providing the necessary materials, scheduling, etc. for successful completion of the project:

_____

_____

_____

_____

_____

_____

_____

_____

_____

_____

_____

_____

_____

4. Pay on time.

One of the most destructive practices in business is delaying payment. Pay on or very close to the day promised or expect it to affect the creative process. Never use the words "the check is in the mail". Do not undertake a project without having the available funds to see it through to completion.

5. Execute the fundamentals of producing power video!!

So many corporate executives do not know what they want, however they seem to know what they **DO NOT** want. Solve this problem before the script is signed off to avoid conflict, delays, and additional expenses. Your budget may limit some frills and expensive 3D graphics in your finished product, so be realistic. If you have chosen the right producer, you will usually be very happy with the results. Your finished project should be very effective provided you simply follow the steps in this **Quick Guide for Producing Powerful Video.**

REMEMBER: There is no "I" in Team!

There is no limit to what can be accomplished if you don't care who gets the credit!

Together Everyone Achieves More!

Use this book to produce your next video. Read with a pen and refer back to each section as you produce. The following note pages are available to help **Produce a Powerful Video.**

Notes:

Notes:

Notes:

Notes:

Notes:

Twelve Week Video and Film Course Available

A twelve week course was created as a precursor for those considering a career in the world of media, film, and associated arts and technologies, and those interested in serving their local churches with media and arts support. Basic technical and production skills are introduced in the classes and supported by technical and philosophical text materials. Coupled with collaborative creative group sessions which are established in the framework of a Christian world-view, students increase their skills while gaining an understanding of the Christian character principles which will insulate and strengthen them from the pitfalls of celebrity and the trappings of the limelight. Whether students are entrepreneurs engaged in secular film careers, media-driven businesses, or church media/arts ministry, this course offers insightful guidelines for achieving fulfilled purpose.

The twelve week course text books are:

How to Succeed in Hollywood (without losing your soul)
 By Dr. Ted Baehr of MovieGuide & the Christian Film & Television Commission

The Articles of Transformation
By Domenic and Charlie Fusco

A Ministry Guide for Producing Powerful Video
(Pre-Production Basics)
By Domenic Fusco

Coursework Outline

Orientation:
1. About FamFlicks: What, Why, Where and When
2. Class Format
3. Website Orientation—Movie Guide Stats.
4. Discussion with Members: What do they Expect and Desire to Accomplish
5. Required Material List
   *Buy "How to Succeed in Hollywood (without losing your soul)" by Ted Baehr
      Read the <u>Preface</u> and <u>Introduction</u>
   **Download: "A Quick Guide for Producing Powerful Video" by Domenic Fusco

Week 1:
1. Core Values Segment: "Core Beliefs vs. Skills" Introduction to The Articles Of Transformation
2. Skills Segment: ** Production Spread Sheet. Ted Baehr's * Chapter 3
3. Project Discussion/Activity: Any Idea where you fit? Your Passion will Place You!

Week 2
1. Core Values Segment: "Absolute Truths for Success"
2. Skills Segment: ** Basic Production Flow for a Movie/Video. Ted Baehr's * Chapter 9
3. Project Discussion/Activity: Pre-production session for Video. Development Phase of a Movie.

Week 3
1. Core Values Segment: Olive Tree - "Vision"
2. Skills Segment: ** Pre-production the Four A's   Ted Baehr's * Chapter 6
3. Project Discussion/Activity. Define the four "A's" for a Movie and Video.

Week 4:
1. Core Values Segment: Olive Tree - "Assets and Liabilities"
2. Skills Segment: ** Basics of screen play writing and video scripts - Ted Baehr's * Chapter 5
3. Project Discussion/Activity: Script writing basics for a feature length Film and Video:

Week 5:
1. Core Values Segment: Olive Tree - "Value of your Beliefs"
2. Skills Segment: Elements in a great script that are necessity for success. Ted Baehr's * Chapter 4.
3. Project Discussion/Activity: Linda Seger, Syd Field,

Week 6:
1. Core Values Segment: Olive Tree - "Expectations"
2. Skills Segment: Branding and image-making
3. Project Discussion/Activity: Samples of Movie Branding. 007 is an Empire.

Week 7:
1. Core Values Segment: Constellations—"The Power of Words" Affirmations
2. Skills Segment: Editing Basics. Non-Linear Software
3. Project Discussion/Activity: Everyone gets to edit. Hands on "Make a Video Presentation"

Week 8:
1. Core Values Segment: Constellations—"The Power of Words" Affirmations Cont'd
2. Skills Segment: Shooting Basics: Dancing and Framing
3. Project Discussion/Activity: Hands on with a camera. Dolly vs. Zoom. Shoot and Capture

Week 9:
1. Core Values Segment: Constellations—"Labors"
2. Skills Segment: Lighting Basics. See the Difference.
3. Project Discussion/Activity: Discuss in detail a Project to be Produced by Group.

Week 10:
1. Core Values Segment: Constellations—"Associations"
2. Skills Segment: The Use of Graphics in Post Production
3. Project Discussion/Activity: Hands on use of canned 3D graphics.

Week 11:
1. Core Values Segment: The Seed—"Decisions Determine Your Destiny"
2. Skills Segment: Directing and Acting. Ted's Book * Chap12 Snap Shots
3. Project Discussion/Activity:

Week 12:
1. Core Values Segment: "Review"
2. Skills Segment: Selling/Marketing Your Idea/Project. Ted Baehr's Chap 8
3. Project Discussion/Activity: Class Interaction. Start to Dream.

About the Author

Domenic Fusco
President and Director/Producer

Domenic Fusco is often called a "Renaissance Man". His educational background is as varied as his life experiences and interests. He holds earned degrees in engineering and theology. His skills in the arts were not cultivated until his mid-twenties when his hobby of photography developed into creating multi-image presentations.

After enjoying a successful career of nineteen years in the electronics industry (R & D engineer, sales rep, sales manager and marketing manager), Domenic leapt out of his career safety net to begin producing media as a full service agency: print, photography, multi-image and video. As a director and producer, he has traveled the globe producing world class projects from concepts to copies. His impressive client base include stars of stage and screen, super models and sports legends, music icons, presidents and kings, corporate leaders and spiritual luminaries.

Domenic Fusco is a contributing author in Solving Ministry's Greatest Problems and co-author of The Articles of Transformation, a seven part character-building series which he shares as a keynote speaker with corporate audiences across the United States. (www.articlesoftransformation.com) Additionally, Domenic has authored three books on media production: The Handbook for Multi-Media Ministry, America's Favorite Video Handbook and The Quick Guide for Producing Powerful Video. These materials have been invaluable for interns Mr. Fusco has taken under his wing over the years, for students at the Art Institute of Atlanta, fledgling production companies, churches and ministries, and as tools to prepare and inform clients about the production process.

Other Works by Domenic Fusco

Nothing Happens Until the Sale is Made
(Book and Audio CD)

"Nothing Happens Until the Sale Is Made" is a must for beginners and a fresh perspective and motivator for the seasoned professional. Mr. Fusco's engaging presentation of the "science" and "relational" philosophy of sales promises the listener an enhanced and educated positioning in the marketplace. Expect to be challenged! Expect to be encouraged! Expect to be propelled toward personal and career successes!

The Articles of Transformation
(Personal Transformation Series Book and Audio CDs)

this eight part series includes:
Treasures Hidden in Plain Sight: An introduction to the timeless principles for personal transformation. *The Olive Tree* exemplifies the foundational character attribute possessed by all who attain true success: Vision. *The Seed* reveals how our destiny is shaped by our Decisions. *The Constellations* course through the heaven's illustrates the character attribute of Discipline. *Fire* is a study in Desire... Its assets and liabilities. The Rose opens our minds to the hidden value of Compassion. *The Diamond* illuminates the path required to develop the character trait of Commitment. *The Butterfly*, creation's most gentle creature, teaches that transformation requires acts of Courage.

www.GreatNewsOnLine.com
(Inspirational Website)

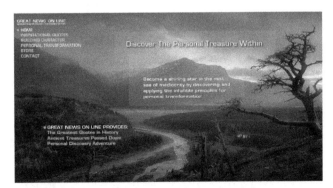

Discover the personal treasure within. Become a shining star in the vast sea of mediocrity. Stay positive, motivated and inspired with free quotes and commentaries. Some of the greaatest achievers in human history will grace you with words of purpose and prosperity.

"You see God always takes the simplest way"
Albert Einstein

CPSIA information can be obtained
at www.ICGtesting.com
Printed in the USA
LVHW101342020419
612673LV00012B/170/P